Sicily Travel Guide

The Most Up-to-Date Pocket Guide to Uncover Sicily's Hidden Treasures | Maximize Your Time and Plan an Unforgettable Adventure in the Jewel of the Mediterranean

Michael Di Paola

Table of Contents

Introduction

The largest Italian island, Sicily, is situated in the Mediterranean Sea near the country's mainland. Its location makes it simple to go to Malta, the coast of North Africa, the Aeolian and Egad Islands, and numerous of Italy's smaller islands.

Sicily is an extreme place. Its environment consists of volcanic peaks, lush, fertile valley meadows, and rocky heights. Under the beautiful Mount Etna, on the rich lava soil, there will be tangy lemon groves.

According to Goethe, "To have seen Sicily without having seen Italy is to have seen Italy not at all." The Sicilian poet's works are adoring tributes to the island's rich cultural history, breathtaking natural beauty, and delicious cuisine.

Ancient Greeks were the first Europeans to settle Sicily, and their rich legacy is visible in the abundance of archaeological finds and superbly maintained ruins. The Temple of Concordia in Agrigento, which is regarded as the most preserved example of a Greek temple in the Doric style anywhere in the world, is the most noteworthy of these. The Cathedral at Monreale and the Palazzo dei Normanni are both outstanding examples of Norman architecture. Although it can be seen in many other locations, the Sicilian Baroque style flourished in cities like Ragusa and Modica.

Sicily offers plenty of spine-tingling thrills, chills, and shivers to offer, especially if you enjoy the macabre. Palermo's monks and aristocrats' mortal remains can be seen up close in the Cappuccini Catacombs, or you can visit Palazzo Chiaramonte to relive the horrors of the Sicilian Inquisition. The almost spotless mummy of two-year-old Rosaria Lombardo is unquestionably the most eerie of these. Visit the well-known theme park at Etnaland for a different kind of excitement that will have you suspended between dizzying heights and fast sinking depths. Visit the Museum of Puppetry to witness the resurgence of a classic Sicilian art form.

When you gaze down on the smoking craters of volcanoes like Mount Etna and Stromboli, get ready to be astounded by the untamed might of nature. The Alcantara Gorge and the mythologically rich Lake Pergusa are two more of Sicily's natural wonders. Bird watchers should prepare their binoculars for a variety of bird species that stop in Sicily on their migratory routes. The Blue Grotto, Isola Bella, and the Egadi Islands are just a few locations that provide excellent opportunity for exploring the underwater world and hiking on undeveloped land. By participating in the olive harvest, sipping Sicilian wine, or observing the operation of the salt pans, you can still feel a connection to the traditional rhythms of the island's way of life.

Chapter 1:
Sicily Travel Basics

When visiting Sicily consider the following:

Best Time to Visit

The best time to visit Sicily depends on your preferences and the activities you plan to engage in. Here's a breakdown of the seasons in Sicily and what they offer:

1. Spring (March to May): One of the best times to visit Sicily is in the spring. With typical temperatures ranging from 15°C (59°F) to 22°C (72°F), the climate is comfortably warm. Flowers are in bloom and the countryside is lush and green, making for a beautiful scene. It's a great time

to go trekking, explore historical places, and engage in other outdoor pursuits.

2. Summer (June to August): Sicily experiences hot, dry summers with regular highs of 30 °C (86 °F). This is a great season to visit coastal places since you can take advantage of the stunning beaches and go swimming in the Mediterranean Sea. Be prepared, nevertheless, for congested tourist spots, particularly in August when many Italians take their vacations.

3. Autumn (September to November): The autumn is still a fantastic season to travel to Sicily. Temperatures are still warm and comfortable, ranging from 18°C (64°F) to 25°C (77°F). As the summer crowds start to thin out, visiting well-liked places becomes simpler. With warm seas for swimming and the extra pleasure of wine and olive harvest festivities, September is very pleasant.

4. Winter (December to February): Sicily's winters are mild by European standards, but the weather can be fickle. With periodic showers of rain, average temperatures range from 10°C (50°F) to 15°C (59°F). If you want to enjoy the island's rich cultural legacy and avoid crowds while visiting historical places, it's an excellent time to go.

In conclusion, spring (March to May) and fall (September to November) are the ideal seasons to visit Sicily because the temperature is milder and there are fewer tourists around.

However, summer can also be nice if you're primarily interested in beach activities and don't mind the high heat.

What to pack

It's critical to pack for a vacation to Sicily by taking the weather, the activities you'll be participating in, and local cultural customs into account. Include the following necessities on your packing list:

1. Clothing:

   - Pack lightweight, loose-fitting garments made of natural materials like cotton or linen because Sicily can grow hot during the summer.
   - Pack your swimsuit because Sicily is home to some stunning beaches.
   - Wearing a sun hat and sunglasses will help you stay safe from the intense Mediterranean sun.
   - Bring appropriate shoes for walking and trekking because Sicily offers many of options for exploration.
   - A lightweight jacket or sweater is advised because evenings can get chilly, especially in the spring and fall.

2. Travel essentials:

- Pack your passport, travel insurance, and any other identification or documentation that may be required.
- Bring some Euro cash, and have a couple other ways to pay on hand, including credit cards.
- Plug adapter: Sicily uses European power outlets, thus if your electronics have a different plug type, you may need an adapter.

3. Toiletries and medications:

- Sunscreen: Shield your skin from the sun's harsh rays. To assist in protecting the local marine habitat, think about packing sunscreen that is reef-safe.
- Mosquito repellent: It's a good idea to have some repellent on hand as mosquitoes can be prevalent, especially in some regions.
- Medications on prescription: Make sure you have enough of any prescription medications you take to last the duration of your vacation.

4. Miscellaneous items:

- Travel guides or maps are helpful because Sicily is full of historical landmarks and tourist sites.
- Reusable water bottle: It's crucial to stay hydrated, especially in hotter areas.
- A daypack or beach bag will be useful for transporting your necessities on day travels or to the beach.

- Whether using a camera or a smartphone, Sicily's breathtaking landscapes and historical landmarks make for fantastic photo possibilities.

Additionally, because English may not be commonly spoken in many places, think about bringing some basic Italian phrases or a language translation tool to help with communication. If you intend to visit religious places, it's also a good idea to research the clothing regulations and customs in the area.

Consider the length of your trip and the accessibility of laundromats when packing lightly and efficiently.

Getting To Sicily and moving around

To get to Sicily, there are several options available depending on your starting point and preferences. Here are some common methods of transportation to Sicily:

1. By Air: Sicily is home to a number of international airports, including Catania and Falcone-Borsellino Airport in Palermo (Fontanarossa Airport). Direct flights are available from several international and major European locations. When you arrive at the airport, you can hire a car or take advantage of various means of transportation to get about the island.
2. By Ferry: You can get to Sicily by ferry if you'd like a beautiful route. Sicily and the rest of Italy are regularly

connected by ferries that stop at ports like Naples, Genoa, Livorno, and Salerno. Depending on the starting place and the preferred boat company, the length of the ferry voyage varies.

3. By Train: You can go to Sicily by train if you're already in Italy. The mainland and Sicily are connected by train services that run via the Strait of Messina. From towns like Rome, Naples, or Reggio Calabria, you may board a train that will transport you to several locations in Sicily.

Once you are in Sicily, you have several options for moving around the island:

- Renting a car is a popular option for seeing Sicily because it offers ease and flexibility. At the airport or in large cities, you can rent a vehicle. However, take in mind that parking and traffic in some places might be difficult, especially in towns like Palermo and Catania.
- Public Transportation: Sicily boasts a robust system of buses and trains for getting about. Within Sicily, buses are a typical means of transportation for getting from town to town. Trains connect the island's various locations as well, however coverage varies by region.
- Taxis and ridesharing services are both prevalent in Sicily, especially in the cities. They are conveniently located in city centers, train terminals, and airports. Some cities also

provide ridesharing services like Uber as a substitute for conventional taxis.

- Guided Trips: If you would like a guided tour, you can sign up for one of the planned tours that visit Sicily's most well-known sights. Travelers will find these tours convenient because they frequently include transportation.

Currency

The Euro (€) is the country's official unit of exchange in both Sicily and the rest of Italy. All transactions in Sicily can be made in Euros, including cash purchases, credit card purchases, and ATM withdrawals.

When visiting Sicily, it's a good idea to have some Euros on hand, especially for smaller businesses or locations that might not accept credit cards. You can use your debit or credit card to withdraw Euros from any of the island's many ATMs.

In general, hotels, restaurants, and larger retail outlets accept major credit cards like Visa, Mastercard, and American Express. But it's always a good idea to keep some cash on hand just in case, especially for smaller shops, neighborhood markets, or transit costs.

To ensure you get a fair exchange rate, it's sometimes advised to exchange money at banks or authorized exchange offices.

Avoid exchanging money at places that aren't authorized or official because they can charge more or give you fake money.

Overall, having Euros on hand will make your trip to Sicily more convenient and enable you to conduct business without difficulty while there.

Language

Since Italian is Sicily's official language, the majority of locals will speak it if you visit as a visitor. It's important to note, too, that the inhabitants also speak a distinctive and lively dialect called Sicilian. Despite having strong Greek, Arabic, and Spanish elements, Sicilian is primarily an Italian language.

In most tourist destinations and big cities like Palermo, Catania, and Taormina, you can get by with Italian, but you can run into locals who speak Sicilian as their primary language in smaller towns and rural areas. The local population's level of English ability might vary, with younger generations typically speaking the language more well.

It's always a good idea to brush up on your Italian before traveling to Sicily as it will improve your interactions with the locals and experience there. Here are some useful Italian expressions you should know:

- Hello: Ciao / Salve (formal)
- Thank you: Grazie
- Please: Per favore
- Excuse me: Mi scusi
- Do you speak English? Parla inglese?
- I don't understand: Non capisco
- Where is...? Dove si trova...?
- How much does it cost? Quanto costa?
- Can you help me? Mi può aiutare?
- Goodbye: Arrivederci

Remember that trying your best to converse in the native tongue, even if it's just a few simple sentences, might help you connect with the Sicilian people and culture.

Cultural Etiquette

It's crucial to understand and respect the local etiquette and culture when visiting Sicily. Sicilians take great pleasure in their traditions and rituals, and they frequently welcome guests who demonstrate an awareness of them. Here are some suggestions for proper cultural behavior for guests in Sicily:

- Greetings: Sicilians value polite greetings. When meeting someone, it's customary to say "buongiorno" (good morning) during the day and "buonasera" (good evening) in the afternoon or evening. Handshakes are common between acquaintances, while close friends and family members may greet each other with hugs or kisses on both cheeks.

- Dress modestly: When visiting churches or other places of worship, Sicilians typically wear conservative attire. In order to show respect, it is advised to cover your shoulders and knees when entering places of worship.
- Punctuality: Sicilian culture has a tendency to be more flexible about timing, therefore being a few minutes late is frequently acceptable. Even so, it's courteous to arrive on time for appointments and meetings. When you've been asked to someone's house, it's normal to be a bit late.
- Dining etiquette: Sicilian food is well-known, and meals play a significant role in the way of life there. It's courteous to accept an invitation to a meal and bring a small present for the host, such as a bottle of wine or some desserts. As soon as the host indicates where you should sit, you should wait to begin your meal. Additionally, as a gesture of gratitude for the food, it's usual to consume everything on your plate.
- Sicily has a significant Catholic background, therefore tourists should show respect for local religious beliefs and customs. Dress appropriately and act in a respectful manner when visiting churches. It's important to ask for permission if you're unsure because taking images might be against the law in some locations.

- Tipping is customary in cafes and restaurants in Sicily. As a rule, if the service was good, it is expected to be tipped between 10% and 15%. Checking the bill is always a good idea, though, as some establishments could add a service fee.

Remember, cultural etiquette can vary from person to person and from one region of Sicily to another. Being respectful, observant, and open-minded will go a long way in ensuring a positive and enjoyable experience while visiting Sicily.

Safety

Although Sicily is generally a safe place to visit, it is always advisable to use the usual safety measures. Watch out for pickpockets and keep a watch on your valuables, especially in busy tourist locations. It's also a good idea to look up travel warnings before your trip.

Chapter 2:
Famous Tourist Attractions In Sicily

The largest island in the Mediterranean Sea, Sicily, is renowned for its extensive history, breathtaking scenery, and rich cultural legacy. The island has a wide range of activities to suit different interests, from historic sites and archaeological digs to lovely beaches and charming villages. The top attractions in Sicily are listed below:

Palermo

Palermo, the capital and largest city of Sicily, is home to about a million people. Palermo draws visitors from all over the world because of its fascinating history, thriving culture, and magnificent architecture. Here are a few of Palermo's tourist-favored attractions:

- Historic Places: Palermo is home to a wide variety of historic places that highlight its rich past. The Royal Tombs are located inside the Palermo Cathedral, commonly called the Cattedrale di Palermo. It is a beautiful example of Arab-Norman architecture. Another must-see location is the Palazzo dei Normanni, often known as the Norman Palace, which is home to the magnificent Palatine Chapel. One of the biggest opera theaters in Europe, the Teatro Massimo, is a magnificent piece of architecture.
- Quattro Canti is a Baroque square in Palermo that serves as the city's center. It is situated at the junction of two major streets. It has four similar Baroque facades that each depict one of the four seasons, a Spanish ruler of Sicily, a patron saint of Palermo, or all three of these things.
- Markets: Palermo is renowned for its thriving street markets, where locals and guests can take in the vivacious ambiance of the city and savor delectable Sicilian street food. The most well-known marketplaces are the Mercato di Ballar, Mercato di Vucciria, and Mercato del Capo, which sell a variety of fresh vegetables, seafood, regional specialties, and handicrafts.
- Via dei Normanni, often known as Norman Street, is bordered by stunning structures and important historical

sites. The Martorana Church, known for its magnificent Byzantine mosaics, is one among the highlights. The Church of San Cataldo, renowned for its striking red domes, is also nearby.

- The Capuchin Catacombs offer a singular experience for people who are interested in horrific history. Mondello Beach: Just a short drive from the city center, Mondello Beach offers a lovely getaway from the urban bustle. These catacombs, located beneath the Capuchin convent, feature thousands of preserved mummies and skeletons dating back several centuries. It is a well-liked location for swimming, sunbathing, and water sports due to its crystal-clear turquoise waters and beautiful white sand.

- Palermo has a number of museums and art galleries that highlight its rich cultural past. An magnificent collection of ancient Sicilian antiquities can be seen in the Regional Archaeological Museum, while the Gallery of Sicilian Art, located in the Palazzo Abatellis, showcases the creations of well-known artists like Antonello da Messina.

- Street Art: Palermo boasts a vibrant street art scene with vibrant murals covering its walls. Particularly well-known for its street art is the Ballar district, where gifted regional and international artists have left their marks on the built environment.

Mount Etna

One of the most well-known and active volcanoes in the world is Mount Etna, which is situated on the east coast of Sicily, Italy. Due to its geological significance, magnificent landscape, and exceptional prospects for exploration and adventure, it draws a sizable number of tourists each year.

Geological Significance:

A stratovolcano, Mount Etna is distinguished by its steep slopes and recurrent explosive eruptions. The tallest active volcano in Europe, at about 3,350 meters (10,990 ft), is this one. The surrounding environment has undergone tremendous change as a result of Etna's volcanic activity, which has been documented for thousands of years. The region's lush greenery and productive agricultural area are a result of the fertile soil that has been formed by the volcanic ash and lava flows.

Breathtaking Scenery:

Visitors are enthralled by Mount Etna's stunning views of its varied environment. A remarkable contrast occurs as you climb the volcano, going from lush woods to arid lava fields. The neighboring coastline, the Ionian Sea, and the lovely cities and villages dotting the region are visible from higher altitudes in panoramic views. Photographers and environment lovers alike are drawn to the stunning sunsets that can be seen from Mount Etna.

Exploration and Adventure:

There are numerous options for exploration and adventure available to visitors to Mount Etna. Visitors can safely explore the volcano's craters, caverns, and lava fields with the help of guided excursions, which are offered. Visitors are transported halfway up the volcano by cable cars and 4x4 vehicles; if the weather is good, they can then trek to the peak. Different levels of fitness and expertise are accommodated on hiking trails of various difficulty.

Skiing and Snowboarding:

Skiers and snowboarders go to Mount Etna throughout the winter to practice their sports. These winter sports have a distinctive setting because to the volcanic terrain. On the volcano, there are ski areas with facilities and ski lifts so that guests can enjoy the slopes and breathtaking views.

Cultural and Historical Significance:

Mount Etna is significant in terms of culture and history in addition to its natural beauty. Local beliefs, folklore, and customs have been impacted by the volcano for millennia. The adjacent towns and villages, like Catania and Taormina, exhibit a synthesis of Sicilian, Roman, and ancient Greek cultures. Visitors can explore historical buildings, theatre from antiquity, and museums to learn more about the area's rich legacy and history.

In conclusion, Mount Etna provides visitors with an enthralling experience by fusing geological significance, stunning beauty, and chances for exploration and adventure. Travelers will find Mount Etna to be a memorable and fascinating trip, whether they choose to see volcanic activity, hike to the peak, ski on its slopes, or immerse themselves in the local culture.

Agrigento

The lovely city of Agrigento is situated on Sicily's southern coast. It is well-known for its extensive history and archaeological sites, which make it a well-liked travel destination for people from all over the world. Here are some of the attractions of Agrigento for tourists:

- Valley of the Temples (Valle dei Templi): The Valley of the Temples, a UNESCO World Heritage Site, is the most well-known site in Agrigento. The ruins of ancient Greek temples can be found in this remarkable archaeological park, and they are exceptionally well maintained. Among the most famous buildings in the valley are the Temple of Concordia, Temple of Juno, and Temple of Hercules.
- The Old Town of Agrigento: The "Kolymbetra," or historic heart of Agrigento, is a picturesque neighborhood with

winding lanes, stunning buildings, and a classic Sicilian vibe. It's a terrific area to explore, find local businesses, and take in the lively culture of the city.

- Scala dei Turchi: This breathtaking natural landmark may be found close to Realmonte, not far from Agrigento. This unusual staircase-like structure drops into the sea from a white marl rock that has been worn by wind and water. The location is well-liked for swimming, shooting, and sunbathing since it has breath-taking vistas.

- Regional Archaeological Museum "Pietro Griffo": This museum is a great resource for learning about the past and present of Agrigento and the region around it. It contains a sizable collection of sculptures, pottery, and architectural remnants from the ancient Greek and Roman civilizations.

- Farm Cultural Park: The Farm Cultural Park in Agrigento is a must-see for everyone with an interest in modern art. It is a vibrant cultural hub located in a neighborhood of restored foreclosed homes. Beaches: Agrigento's coastline location allows access to stunning beaches along the Mediterranean Sea. The park displays contemporary art works, holds events, exhibitions, and performances, and serves as a platform for local and international artists. San Leone is a well-known beach resort region with sandy shoreline, clean waters, and a lively nightlife that is just a few kilometers from the city center.

- Festivals & Events: Agrigento holds a number of festivals and events all year long that highlight the customs and history of the area. The Almond Blossom Festival, which takes place in February, welcomes spring with vibrant parades, ethnic music, and regional foods. The Greek Theatre Festival, which takes place in the summer, features theatrical productions in Agrigento's historic Greek Theater.

Ragusa

In Sicily, Italy, there is a wonderful city called Ragusa. Ragusa Superiore (Upper Ragusa) and Ragusa Ibla, the older and more scenic section of the city, are the two sections that make up the whole. Ragusa is well-known for its mouthwatering cuisine, UNESCO World Heritage Sites, and gorgeous Baroque architecture. Let's look at some of Ragusa's tourism attractions:

- Any traveler should visit the historic district of Ragusa Ibla. Its picturesque cathedrals, palaces, and winding lanes serve as a display for the city's extensive architectural history. The magnificent Cathedral of San Giorgio, a renowned example of Sicilian Baroque architecture, is located in Ragusa Ibla's central square, Piazza Duomo.
- Ragusa Superiore: Although Ragusa's higher region is more contemporary, it yet retains a certain allure. Corso Italia, the main street, has a bustling environment with

stores, cafes, and restaurants. You can get a bird's eye view of Ragusa Ibla from Ragusa Superiore.

- Donnafugata Castle: This lovely sight is close to Ragusa and is located there. This old castle, which is surrounded by beautiful grounds, provides a window into the area's aristocratic history. Additionally, it has appeared in films and television shows.
- Iblean Gardens: These well-kept gardens are located on Ragusa Ibla's historic walls. They offer a tranquil haven where you may unwind and take in the stunning views of the surrounding countryside.
- Foodie Highlights: Ragusa is well known for its delicious cuisine. Arancini (stuffed rice balls), cannoli (sweet pastry tubes filled with ricotta), and pasta alla Norma (pasta with eggplant, tomato sauce, and ricotta salata cheese) are some of the classics from Sicily that you simply must try.
- The Church of Santa Maria delle Scale in Ragusa is yet another stunning specimen of Baroque design. It is renowned for its elaborate interior and magnificent staircase that rises to the entryway.
- The Museum of Ragusa, which is situated in Ragusa Superiore, is home to a variety of archaeological objects, historical relics, and works of art that shed light on the history and culture of the area.
- Scicli: Another UNESCO-listed Baroque town worth seeing is Scicli, which is located near to Ragusa. Beautiful

churches and palaces can be found there, such as the Church of San Matteo and the Palazzo Beneventano.

- Beaches: Although not located in Ragusa itself, there are lovely beaches close by. Popular seaside resort Marina di Ragusa is renowned for its white sands and blue waters.
- Festivals: Throughout the year, Ragusa hosts a number of festivals, including religious processions, cuisine festivals, and customary celebrations. The Infiorata di San Giorgio, when the streets of Ragusa Ibla are covered in elaborate floral carpets, is one prominent occasion.

Syracuse

Syracuse, usually referred to as Siracusa, is a historic city situated on Sicily's eastern coast. Syracuse is a well-liked travel destination for travellers looking to experience its historical sites, picturesque neighborhoods, and stunning coastline regions. Syracuse has a long history that dates back to antiquity. The following features of Syracuse make it a must-see destination for tourists:

- Ancient Greek and Roman Ruins: Syracuse, which is home to UNESCO World Heritage Sites, is well known for its well-preserved ancient Greek and Roman ruins. The Parco Archeologico della Neapolis is home to the spectacular Greek Theater, the Roman Amphitheater, and the Ear of Dionysius, a limestone cave renowned for its acoustics, making it the most well-known site.

- The historic core of Syracuse is located on Ortigia Island, which is connected to the mainland by bridges. It is a delightful island with winding lanes, ornate buildings, and lovely piazzas. The majestic Syracuse Cathedral, which was constructed on the site of an ancient temple, is located on the Piazza Duomo, the city's central plaza.

- The Syracuse Cathedral, sometimes referred to as the Duomo di Siracusa, is a magnificent illustration of Baroque design. The cathedral has ruins of an Arab mosque and Doric columns from a Greek temple, among other artifacts from many historical eras.

- The Fountain of Arethusa is a natural spring that is the subject of numerous myths. It is situated on Ortigia Island. Greek legend holds that the nymph Arethusa changed into a spring in order to flee the advances of the river god

Alpheus. The fountain is a serene location with lovely sea views.

- Castello Maniace is a medieval fortification with sweeping views of the city and the sea that is located on the easternmost point of Ortigia Island. The majestic Castello Maniace, which dates back to the 13th century, has been used for many different things throughout its history, including as a royal home and a fortification.

- The Catacombs of San Giovanni are historic cemeteries that date back to the early Christian era, and they are conveniently located just outside the city. The early Christian frescoes and graves are visible in the tunnels below ground, which are open for exploration.

- Syracuse Museums: Syracuse is home to a number of museums that display its ancient riches and provide light on its extensive past. The most prominent museum is the Museo Archeologico Regionale Paolo Orsi, which has a huge collection of relics from Sicily, Rome, and ancient Greece.

- Syracuse is endowed with breathtaking beaches and coastal vistas. Beautiful hiking trails, waterfalls, and natural swimming holes are all present in the close-by Riserva Naturale Orientata Cavagrande del Cassibile.

- Festivals: Throughout the year, Syracuse conducts a number of events, such as the Greek Theater Festival in May and June, which features plays by the ancient Greeks presented at the city's historic theater. Another significant holiday, the Feast of Saint Lucy, is observed in December and is marked by religious processions and pyrotechnics.

- Local cuisine: Syracuse has a vast selection of delectable foods, including some of the world-famous Sicilian cuisine. Try some of the regional seafood specialties like grilled swordfish or pasta with fresh clams, as well as authentic Sicilian desserts like cannoli and cassata.

With its blend of history, culture, stunning landscapes, and delicious food, Syracuse provides a memorable experience for tourists seeking a taste of ancient and modern Sicily.

Catania

On Sicily's eastern coast, in Italy, is the lovely city of Catania. It is renowned for its extensive past, beautiful architecture, vibrant culture, and close vicinity to Mount Etna, one of the world's most active volcanoes. As a result, Catania draws a sizable number of visitors who come to see its landmarks and take in its distinctive ambiance.

The medieval city center of Catania, which is a UNESCO World Heritage Site, is one of the city's top attractions. The city center is distinguished by its elaborate churches, palaces, and squares that are examples of Baroque architecture. The Piazza del Duomo, where the magnificent Catania Cathedral is located, is the most well-known square in Catania. The cathedral is a must-see destination and is devoted to St. Agatha, the city's patron saint.

The Ursino Castle, a 13th-century fortification, is another significant location in Catania. The Civic Museum, which displays a variety of relics and objects illustrating Catania's history and culture, is presently housed in the castle.

The Fera o Luni, a bustling street market, is another popular attraction in Catania. Fresh produce, fish, cheeses, and traditional Sicilian fare are among the local goods sold in this thriving market. It's a wonderful location to experience the local culture and sample some traditional Sicilian cuisine.

A trip to Mount Etna is strongly advised for everyone who is interested in learning more about Catania's natural environment. For those who enjoy the outdoors, this active volcano provides numerous hiking trails and breath-taking views. The volcano's crater can be explored and its geological significance learned about through guided excursions.

Catania is renowned for its vibrant nightlife scene as well. There are numerous taverns, clubs, and eateries in the city where guests may dance, take in live music, and savor delectable Sicilian fare.

An international airport makes Catania easily reachable for travelers from all over the world in terms of transportation. Additionally, the city boasts an effective public transit system, which includes buses and a metro line, making it simple to go around and explore.

Overall, Catania is a desirable travel destination because it offers a distinctive fusion of history, culture, and natural beauty. Every visitor may find something to do in Catania, whether they want to take in the ancient attractions, the lively local scene, or the natural surroundings.

Taormina

On Sicily's eastern coast, Taormina is a lovely town in Italy. It is renowned for its breathtaking natural beauty, lengthy history, and extensive cultural heritage. Taormina has long been a well-liked vacation spot and still draws tourists from all over the world today. Let's talk about some of the attractions that make Taormina a must-see destination for travelers.

- The Greek-Roman theater in Taormina is without a doubt the city's most recognizable landmark. It provides stunning views of Mount Etna and the Sicilian coastline and was constructed in the third century BC. Concerts, operas, and other cultural events are still held in the theater today, which adds to its distinctive charm.

- Corso Umberto: The main thoroughfare in Taormina, Corso Umberto, is a hive of activity. It provides tourists with a great experience as they explore and engage in shopping and dining. It is lined with shops, cafes, restaurants, and boutiques. The Boulevard also boasts stunning architecture and scenic surroundings.

- Isola Bella is a little island natural reserve that is only a short distance from Taormina and is only accessible by a short stretch of sand. Visitors looking for relaxation and the beauty of nature are drawn to its spotless beach and its clean waves. Botanical gardens and a small museum are also located on the island.

- Ancient Ruins: Taormina is home to a number of intriguing ancient ruins. Both the Naumachia, a sizable archaeological site containing the ruins of a Roman naval battle arena, and the Odeon, a modest Roman theater, provide insights into the town's past. These locations offer an insight of Taormina's function in prehistoric times.

- Taormina is renowned for its exquisitely designed gardens and parks. A tranquil haven with vibrant flowers, fountains, and sweeping views is the Villa Comunale. The Garden at Villa Carlotta gives breathtaking views of the coastline while showcasing a range of subtropical plants.

- Festivals and Events: Taormina organizes a number of festivals and cultural events every year. International film stars and a variety of cinematic works are included at the Taormina Film Festival, which takes place every June. Theater, music, and dance performances are featured during the Taormina Arte festival, further enhancing the cultural landscape.
- Local Cuisine: Sicilian food is well-known across the world, and Taormina has a good selection of eateries where tourists may sample traditional fare. For food lovers, the local gastronomy is a highlight, offering everything from excellent pastries and gelato to fresh seafood.

In conclusion, Taormina is a captivating destination that combines stunning natural landscapes, ancient history, cultural treasures, and a vibrant atmosphere. Whether you're interested in exploring ancient ruins, lounging on beautiful beaches, or immersing yourself in the local culture, Taormina has something to offer every tourist.

Trapani and the Salt Pans

On Sicily's western coast, Trapani is a compelling city renowned for its deep history, beautiful architecture, and gorgeous natural scenery. The Salt Pans, often referred to as Saline di Trapani e Paceco, are one of the most well-known tourist destinations in Trapani. These salt pans, which have been in use for many years, give visitors a fascinating look at the old-fashioned method of making salt.

Along the coastline, the Salt Pans of Trapani are a collection of salt marshes and shallow lagoons. The network of canals and windmills that make up this gorgeous environment were previously employed to speed up the evaporation and salinity collection processes. A key cultural and economic emblem of the area, the salt pans still use ancient methods to generate high-quality sea salt today.

Visitors to the Salt Pans of Trapani can stroll along designated routes or join guided tours to learn more about the region. These excursions offer an intriguing look into the numerous steps in the production of salt, from the gathering of saltwater to the ultimate harvesting of salt crystals. Visitors can watch the evaporation procedure, in which seawater is directed into a number of pans where it slowly evaporates to produce crystallized salt.

The Salt Pans of Trapani are notable for their historical and cultural value, but they also provide breathtaking views and interesting photo opportunities. A fascinating visual spectacle is produced by the juxtaposition of the dazzling white salt pans and the deep blue Mediterranean Sea. The area's windmills, which offer a view of the traditional equipment employed in salt production, contribute to its allure.

Tourists can visit the Salt Museum (Museo del Sale) in Trapani in addition to exploring the salt pans. This museum offers more details on the background and significance of salt production in the area by showing old artifacts, pictures, and hands-on displays. Visitors can have a thorough experience there while learning about the Salt Pans of Trapani's cultural legacy.

Additionally, there are other tourist sites in Trapani proper. The spectacular San Lorenzo Cathedral and the Church of Purgatorio are only two examples of the city's magnificent Baroque architecture. The old district of Trapani is a labyrinth of winding streets and lovely squares filled with quaint boutiques, cafes, and eateries. The city is a well-liked destination for beach lovers and fans of water sports due to its coastal location.

Trapani is a great starting point for seeing the Egadi Islands and other local sights. These lovely islands, which include Favignana, Levanzo, and Marettimo, have breathtaking beaches, clean waters, and diving and snorkeling opportunities.

Travelers seeking a mix of historical, scenic, and cultural activities can definitely visit Trapani and its Salt Pans. While the city itself boasts a variety of architectural gems and maritime beauty, the Salt Pans offer a unique look at the traditional salt production process. Trapani and the Salt Pans are certain to make an impression, whether you are interested in history, photography, or simply the Mediterranean atmosphere.

Cefalù

On Sicily's northern coast, in Italy, sits the lovely seaside town of Cefalù. It is a well-liked vacation spot renowned for its magnificent beaches, charming neighborhoods, and rich history. Here are some of Cefalù's top attractions for visitors:

- The Cefalù Cathedral, often referred to as the Cathedral Basilica of Cefalù, is the town's most recognizable feature. This magnificent cathedral, built in the 12th century in the Norman-Arabic style, has spectacular architecture and delicate mosaics.
- La Rocca: The enormous rock feature known as La Rocca dominates Cefalù. The town and the nearby shoreline may be seen in exquisite detail from the summit, which is a popular trekking destination.
- Historic Center: Cefalù's historic center is a lovely region with meandering, little lanes, historic structures, and a lively ambiance. Visitors can explore nearby stores, cafes, and restaurants while taking in the medieval atmosphere by strolling through the town's lanes.
- Cefalù Beach: The town is home to a lovely sandy beach that draws tourists and water sports lovers. It's the perfect location for swimming, sunbathing, and engaging in other water activities thanks to the crystal-clear turquoise waters and attractive surroundings.

- Mandralisca Museum: The Mandralisca Museum is a must-see destination for everyone with an interest in art or history. The museum is home to a sizable collection of artworks, historical relics, and a well-known picture by Antonello da Messina called "Portrait of an Unknown Sailor."
- Medieval Lavatoio: A few of Cefalù's "lavatoio," or medieval lavatories, have survived. These old buildings, which were previously public laundry rooms, are now fascinating landmarks that provide light on the town's past.
- Festivals & Events: Throughout the year, Cefalù holds a number of festivals and events that draw both residents and visitors. The Festival of Saint Salvatore, which takes place on August 13 and includes fireworks, processions, and cultural acts, is the most well-known festival.
- Local Cuisine: Cefalù offers the chance to sample the delectable flavors of the world-famous Sicilian cuisine. In the town's restaurants and trattorias, visitors can savor fresh seafood, pasta dishes, arancini (stuffed rice balls), cannoli (Italian pastries), and other culinary treats.

Overall, Cefalù offers a perfect blend of history, natural beauty, and cultural experiences, making it an enchanting destination for tourists seeking relaxation, exploration, and immersion in Sicilian traditions.

The Aeolian Islands

The Aeolian Islands, often referred to as the Lipari Islands, are a charming archipelago that can be found in the Tyrrhenian Sea off the Italian island of Sicily's northeastern coast. Lipari, Vulcano, Salina, Stromboli, Filicudi, Alicudi, and Panarea are the seven major islands that make up this magnificent collection of volcanic islands. Here are the islands' top attractions and the reasons why people travel there.

1. Lipari: The Aeolian archipelago's largest and most populous island, Lipari is a well-liked starting point for travels around the area. It has attractive towns, stunning coastlines, and an intriguing archaeological museum on the site of the old Acropolis.

2. Volcano: This island is well-known for its lava flows and healing mud baths. The island's major volcanic crater, the Gran Cratere, is accessible by hiking, and once there, visitors can unwind and rejuvenate in the warm mud baths.

3. Salina: Salina is renowned for its wineries, picturesque scenery, and lush flora. Visitors can go on wine tasting trips and discover the quaint villages of Santa Marina and Malfa. The island is known for its delicious Malvasia wine.

4. One of the most well-known islands in the Aeolian archipelago is Stromboli, an active volcano that provides visitors with a singular experience. Visitors may watch the

volcano's magnificent outbursts and take in breath-taking vistas of the surrounding waters by hiking to the volcano's top.

5. The two islands of Filicudi and Alicudi are the most remote and undeveloped in the archipelago, making them perfect for travelers looking for a quiet getaway and a taste of island life in the past. Both islands provide breathtakingly beautiful natural scenery, pristine waterways, and a serene atmosphere.

6. Panarea: Also referred to as the "VIP island," this gorgeous location is popular with the jet-set population. It provides posh resorts, hip eateries, and a buzzing nightlife. Beautiful beaches and secret coves on the island are ideal for swimming and tanning.

In addition to the distinctive qualities of each island, the Aeolian Islands as a whole provide a variety of outdoor recreation opportunities and scenic splendor. To explore the marine life, underwater caverns, and rock formations, tourists can go swimming, snorkeling, scuba diving, and on boat trips. In addition to offering plenty of options for hiking and exploring gorgeous routes, the islands' pristine seas make them perfect for those who enjoy participating in water sports.

Because of their exceptional natural beauty, volcanic activity, and special relationship between man and nature, the Aeolian Islands have been included on the UNESCO World Heritage List. The

Aeolian Islands are a riveting experience for all kinds of travelers, whether you're looking for relaxation, adventure, or cultural exploration.

Erice

On the Italian island of Sicily, in the Trapani region, sits the lovely medieval town of Erice. The village, which is perched atop Mount Erice at a height of around 750 meters (2,460 feet), provides breath-taking views over the area's landscape, coastline, and the nearby Egadi Islands. The well-preserved medieval center, extensive cultural history, and various tourist attractions make Erice a well-known destination. Let's examine some of Erice's main tourist destinations and highlights:

- The medieval fortification known as Castello di Venere (Castle of Venus) gives sweeping views of the town and the shoreline. It's a well-liked location to take in the sunset or the breathtaking views of the surroundings.
- Known as the Chiesa Matrice (Mother Church), Erice's main church is a stunning example of Norman design. Beautiful works of art and religious artifacts can be found inside.
- Erice's emblem is the Torretta Pepoli, a medieval tower also referred to as the Clock Tower. Visit the Museum of Popular Arts and Traditions located inside the tower after ascending to the top for breathtaking views.

- Giardino del Balio (Balio Gardens): With well-kept grass, vibrant flowers, and shaded pathways, these verdant gardens offer a tranquil respite. It's the perfect location for a picnic or leisurely stroll.
- The Assumption of the Virgin Mary is the focus of the Erice Cathedral, sometimes referred to as the Duomo. Explore the interior, which features important artworks, and admire the building's stunning exterior.
- The Streets of Erice: Erice's meandering, congested streets make for a lovely stroll. Beautiful buildings, little stores selling regional crafts and specialties, and pleasant cafes adorn the streets.
- Visit Pasticceria Maria Grammatico, a renowned pastry business in Erice that is well-known for its almond pastries. Try some mouthwatering cannoli, marzipan fruits, and other typical Sicilian delicacies.
- Taking a cable car will get you to Erice from the foot of Mount Erice. It's an easy method to get to the hilltop location and the journey offers beautiful views as you ascend to the town.
- Festival of Ancient Music: If you travel to Erice in July, you might be able to take part in this event. This festival honors classical music from various historical eras and is held at a number of locations around the city.
- Cooking classes: Erice is renowned for its cuisine, so taking a cooking class is a great way to get a taste of the regional

fare. Discover how to make typical Sicilian foods including couscous, caponata, and cassata.

Noto

The Italian island of Sicily's eastern coast is home to the city of Noto. It has been recognized as a UNESCO World Heritage Site and is highly known for its exquisite Baroque architecture. To distinguish it from the nearby modern city of Noto, the settlement is frequently referred to as Noto Antica.

An enormous earthquake that occurred in 1693 completely destroyed the once-thriving town of Noto Antica. The spectacular architectural ensemble that tourists may see now is the product of the city's reconstruction in the Sicilian Baroque style following the catastrophe. A distinctive and endearing ambiance is produced by the buildings in Noto, which include beautiful facades, detailed craftsmanship, and majestic palaces.

Some of the notable landmarks in Noto include:

- The majestic Noto Cathedral, also known as the Cattedrale di San Nicol, stands as the city's main landmark. It has an amazing front with ornate ornamentation and statuary.
- In honor of the patron saint of the city, Palazzo Ducezio is a palace that is situated in the center of Noto. It is a magnificent illustration of Sicilian Baroque architecture and is used as the town hall right now.

- San Domenico Church: This church beautifully exemplifies Noto's Baroque style. It has a lovely curved façade with fine carvings and ornamentation.
- One of the most well-known structures in Noto is the Palazzo Nicolaci, which is renowned for its magnificent balconies. The balconies offer breathtaking views of the city and are decorated with beautiful wrought-iron work.

Noto offers a wide range of cultural and culinary events in addition to its architectural marvels. Infiorata di Noto, a well-known flower festival held in May in the city, has elaborate flower carpets lining the streets. Additionally, tourists can savor the delectable Sicilian food, which features regional delicacies like cannoli, arancini, and granita.

When you explore the neighborhood, you'll come upon the magnificent Vendicari Nature Reserve, which features spectacular beaches, wetlands, and wildlife. Another beautiful natural area is the Cavagrande del Cassibile nature reserve, which has hiking paths, waterfalls, and canyons.

In conclusion, Noto is a fascinating location for tourists interested in Sicilian culture, history, and Baroque architecture. It is a must-see location in Sicily because of its preserved buildings, rich heritage, and stunning landscapes.

Chapter 3:

Weather and Activities in Sicily

Most tourists looking for peace and quiet travel to Sicily to take advantage of the island's pristine waters, go hiking on picturesque trails, and take leisurely strolls through the charming Baroque neighborhoods of its historic cities. Even while this is the typical Sicilian tourist experience, there is still a ton to do in the off-season for travelers seeking lower prices or a more inside experience.

It might be beneficial to brave the city's busiest travel season in order to enjoy a holiday in Sicily that includes lounging in the sun, swimming in the Mediterranean, seeing the city's vibrant neighborhoods, shopping at open-air markets, and hiking comfortably in lovely weather. The beauty of Sicily's outdoor attractions is certainly worth it, even if you have to share it with other visitors.

The finest months for sightseeing are from mid-April to mid-June or from mid-September to mid-October in Sicily. Even though it will be sunny and warm at these times, there won't likely be as many tourists as there would be in July and August, the two busiest summer months. If you want to avoid the rain, go in the spring. No matter when you intend to visit, all state-run museums, galleries, parks, gardens, and ruins are free to enter on the first Sunday of every month throughout the entire year.

The official beach season, which begins in June and is also when the majority of tourists arrive, is the finest time to visit Sicily's beaches.

Come in May since it's usually warm enough for swimming, especially in the second half of the month, if you want to enjoy the sea without the crowds. By September and frequently October, the sea won't have cooled much, but by then, a lot of tourists will have left.

January

In Sicily, January is also the wettest month of the year. The wet weather is nonetheless accompanied by the start of Carnival season, fewer travelers, and lower costs than during other times of the year. This is also one of the best winter months for a little skiing on the slopes of Mount Etna.

Weather

The average temperature in coastal cities like Palermo is 54 °F (12 °C), but when the sirocco winds blow, it may get as hot as 68 °F (20 °C). This is one of the wettest and coldest times of year to travel to Sicily. Despite Sicily as a whole having pleasant, generally sunny weather with over 18 days of rain, the island's climate differs. Along the seaside, the climate is Mediterranean. It's likely that the winter will be mild and rainy.

Contrarily, Messina is a few degrees warmer and has its own microclimate. Sicily's rugged interior has colder temperatures and a danger of snow. The cold and slopes with enough snow anywhere above 3,300 feet (1000 m) draw skiers and snowboarders.

Something to Do

Enjoy a tranquil month of cultural discovery after the Epiphany, which concludes the Christmas season (barring Carnivale if it lands in January). Renting a car is the most convenient way to move around the city. If it starts to rain, go inside one of the numerous museums or art galleries that are available. for beautiful artworks from the medieval and Renaissance eras to the present.

Several cities and villages on the Italian island have ancient geothermal hot springs where you can unwind for the afternoon. Visit Sciacca or the warm springs in Terme Segestane, which are supposed to be the spot where the Nymphs of Greek myth tried to heal Hercules. Terme Segestane is close to Castellammare del Golfo. Alternatively, after a day of skiing or snowboarding, spend the evening warming up in a bathhouse at Santa Venera al Pozzo, which is close to Acireale.

February

In February, when almond trees are in bloom in the south and there are many activities going on, Sicily's brief winter comes to an end. At this time, the island's highest peaks are still blanketed in snow. Additionally, prices are lower, and there are less tourists. Sicily, which has a sizable Catholic population, is happy throughout Lent, Carnivale, and Mardi Gras, which is celebrated all over the country to commemorate the beginning of spring.

Weather

With average high temperatures of 42–54°F (5–12°C) throughout the island and 48–59°F (9–15°C) in Palermo, Sicily has little change from January to February, but the amount of rain continues to decline. The temperature around the coasts will be milder than inland and will also see slightly more rain, despite the hilly side experiencing cooler weather, such as Prizzi, with an average range of 36-46°F (2-8°C). Higher elevations like Mount

Etna will be cooler, but skiers will be drawn to their resorts by their snow-covered flanks.

Additionally, coastal temperatures could momentarily near freezing if breezes from the Balkan Peninsula are present. With all of that, heading to the beach to relax in the erratic sun is not unusual. Simply avoid the water (59°F/15°C).

Something to Do

In February, it's a great time to be flexible and see the local atmosphere. Utilize the listings for house rentals or agriturismos to stay a few days on a farm and revel in seeing local life with few other visitors in the area (renting a car is your best option for this experience).

While the weather is still cool and keeping away foreign tourists, explore Sicily's extensive collection of historical sites, medieval towns, and baroque city centers. Explore the Valley of the Temples in Agrigento, the Greek theater from Syracuse's Neapolis Archaeological Park, and the winding alleyways of Ragusa Ibla, Modica, and Scicli for outstanding examples of Sicilian Baroque architecture.

The opera season officially begins this month, and notable performances will be held at several illustrious sites. One such theater, which also happens to be the largest in Italy, is Teatro Massimo in Palermo. And if you ever find yourself in the regional capital, go for a stroll through the sparkling grid of saline basins at Trapani's salt flats. It's especially beautiful at sunset.

March

Spring has blossomed along the coast for those who want to see it all, while Mount Etna and the mountains are still blanketed in snow. Because there are less tourists and housing and airfare costs are still reasonable, now is the ideal time to travel to well-known locations without the crowds or to go outside and go hiking, bicycling, or skiing.

Weather

Sicily's brief winter season comes to an end in March as the weather begins to warm up, with average highs and lows of 59 F (15 C) and 43 F (6 C), respectively. The water is still too chilly for swimming at 59 F (15 C).

While coastal communities in the north, west, and south, including Palermo, Marsala, and Agrigento, have milder temperatures and less rain than Messina, Catania, and Syracuse do (wet enough to see things bloom and become green, but not enough to spoil your holiday).

March is generally dreary with rain, wind, and thunderstorms, however there may be a few sunny days. Along with a few additional layers of clothes and damp gear, pack your sunglasses.

Something to Do

Even though it's probably not warm enough for a beach vacation, it's a perfect time to go hiking or cycling because the weather gets warmer and dryer toward the end of the month. The spring season will also have arrived on the island because wildflowers will start to bloom, and farmers will start tilling the ground. Starting your exploration of Sicily's numerous amazing hiking and cycling trails at Mount Etna is a great idea.

Even though climbers are only allowed to ascend to a height of 9,500 feet (the peak's highest point is 11,000 feet), there is plenty of volcanic activity evident from 6,500 feet up in the Silvestri Crater. There are options to take a cable car or a four-wheel-drive vehicle if you'd like to take a break throughout the six-hour trip. If biking is your preferred sport, you have countless possibilities.

Ortygia, the historic center of Syracuse, is a great place to go touring right now because you can go into a museum or café whenever the mood strikes. For a unique experience, go to the Ipogei di Piazza Duomo, a system of underground tunnels utilized during World War II. Another intriguing underground option is to visit the fabled Miqweh, or Jewish baths. When the Jewish residents were compelled to leave in the late 15th century, these baths were shut off for a protracted period of time.

April

The Italian Island is lush, verdant, and strewn with blossoming citrus fruit as the entire country descends for Easter celebrations. During this off-peak month, take advantage of the lower prices and fewer visitors to get outside and experience everything that Sicily has to offer.

Weather

As the temperature rises in April, the days progressively get longer. The typical daily temperature in Sicily ranges from 8 to 16 degrees Celsius (46 to 60 degrees Fahrenheit), so you should bring warmer clothing for the evenings. The capital of Sicily, Palermo, typically experiences temperatures between 52- and 66-degrees Fahrenheit (11.9 to 19 degrees Celsius), while it gets more hotter and drier between Syracuse and Catania.

Keep your sunglasses and umbrella handy and layer your clothing to be prepared for any weather. If you plan to do skiing or snowboarding, it is best to plan your trip for the north side of Mount Etna and to bring appropriate warm clothing. Even though the sea is still a little chilly (61°F/15°C), the days may be sunny and warm enough for a beach setting, so bring your swimwear, nonetheless.

Something to Do

On Mount Etna's northern slopes, you might still be able to fit in a few short-sleeved runs even if the ski season is coming to an end (if it hasn't already) (Linguaglossa). If winter activities aren't your thing in April, the island is open to beachgoers, hikers, and bikers who want to take advantage of the mild weather, sparse crowds, and blooming wildflowers. If you're short on time, consider hiking up to Torre del Filosofo rather than signing up for a guided trek to the summit of Mount Etna. At a height of 9,500 feet, you may still enjoy island panoramas and get a glimpse of Europe's largest volcano (2,900 m).

Of course, there are a ton of additional trekking options to consider, like the popular beach walk in the Zingaro Natural Reserve or the more difficult climb and scramble paths on Monte Cofano. Renting a car or a bike is another creative way to see the many Sicilian landscapes. A challenging 33-mile route that starts and ends in the charming city of Cefalù and takes you up into mountain settlements with views of the Tyrrhenian Sea is the Sicilia Dag 7.

Visit Trapani at the Festival del Vento if you prefer water sports like sailing, kayaking, wind and kite surfing (Wind Festival). Landlubbers will find a lot to enjoy in the city, such as culinary contests and tastings, live performances, such as dance and theater, and street performers. There are also many other Sagre for foodies to choose from, such as the Artichoke Festival in Cerda, the Sagra della Ricotta e dei Formaggio in Sampieri, which celebrates Sicilian cheeses, and the Ricotta Festival in Vizzini, which is celebrated for its ricotta cheese, which is popular throughout Sicily.

If you're in the southeast of the island, you should eat Easter lamb in Syracuse before going to Modica, a UNESCO-listed baroque jewel of a town where you should try the special Mpanatigghi sweets sold at Easter. Modica is renowned for its winding staircases and confusing alleyways.

May

May is without a doubt one of the best months to travel abroad and visit Sicily. The weather is consistently lovely, people aren't overly busy, and there are many delicious and enjoyable festivals to attend, so you may tour the Italian island at your leisure.

Weather

May in Sicily delivers more daylight hours and generally pleasant weather. By the middle of the month, the water may be 65°F (19°C) warm enough to tempt daring swimmers.

In Sicily, Palermo, Marsala, and Agrigento can see 73 °F (23 °C) daily average highs, while Catania and Syracuse can experience

75 °F (54 °C). In Sicily, daily average temperatures range from 12 to 19 °C, or 53 to 67 °F.

On Mount Etna's peak, snow is still visible even though ski season has ended. So keep in mind that the temperature will decrease as you ascend. Bring warmer layers, shorts, and t-shirts, as well as layers for those cooler evenings and higher altitudes.

Something to Do

Without a doubt, May is one of the best months to travel to Sicily. Without the throngs that peak season brings, take advantage of some of the island's best beaches. Excellent options include the beaches on the east coast villages of Mazzaro and Marina di Ragusa, San Vito lo Capo, which is close to Trapani, and Mondello, which is located close to Palermo. Take a ferry to the Aegadi Islands from Marsala or Trapani to enjoy the beautiful beaches there, including Favignana's Cala Rosa for something a little more private.

Before the summer crowds flood the islands and the sun is at its worst, think about going to the Aeolian Islands for some hiking, especially on Stromboli and Salina. A moderately challenging 2.5-mile (4-kilometer) journey will take you to Fossa delle Felci, the highest point in Salina. Alternatively, you can climb Stromboli's active volcano to see eruptions. Additionally, since Salina is the Aeolian Island that does the least environmental harm, you might wish to reward yourself to some of the region's locally produced Malvasia wine.

To view flamingos eating, nature lovers may choose to try their luck in the Vendicari Nature Reserve's saltwater lagoons. Even if the pink birds aren't there, the trip to the southeast won't be in useless because the region has beautiful white sand beaches and walking options. Discover more hiking and trekking alternatives in the hills while the flowers are in bloom, such as in the Madonie and Nebrodi mountains in northern Sicily.

June

Sicily begins to heat up in June, and travelers flock to the region's coastline and well-known cultural sites because of the great beach weather. Even though you'll have to contend with the crowds, there are numerous options from which you can choose to create the ideal island vacation.

Weather

Sicily's climate, with daily highs and lows of 74 F (23 C) and 60 F (15 C), is consistently nice enough to entice visitors to the beaches along the coast. Bring beach clothing and a lightweight sweater for the cool evenings. If you're intending to travel inland, be aware that without the sea's cooling effect, temperatures may be higher in the first 1,000 to 1,500 feet. Ragusa, for example, experiences temperatures between 16 and 29 °C (61 and 84 °F).

When the sirocco (a scorching African breeze) blows on such hot days, the sea is even more inviting at 72 degrees Fahrenheit (22 degrees Celsius). In Messina, the hottest days can reach 109°F (43°C), while Trapani, Palermo, and Catania can reach 111°F (44°C).

Something to Do

June is a great month for cultural touring even though the major sites start to feel crowded toward the end of the month. The sea is finally warm enough for swimming and all other water-related activities (kayaking, kite/windsurfing, sailing, snorkeling/scuba diving), making the coast and the islands the perfect vacation destinations. Three beaches that are less busy include Porto Palo, which is south of Menfi, Sampieri, which is southeast of Scicli, and Letojanni, which is north of Taormina.

The Madonie and Nebrodi mountains are another fantastic site to explore, and there are many different hiking and walking trails there. Consider the 44-mile (70-km) route that passes by lakes, the Etna wine region, mountain passes, and valleys while planning your mountain riding excursion. You can also go body rafting or go on a river hike via the Alcantara River and Gorge when you're on this part of the island.

July

Without a doubt, Sicily experiences its busiest month for tourism in July. Throughout the month and all around the island, there are a lot of fun and interesting cultural and musical activities. The Mediterranean is welcoming and friendly, and the weather is mild and sunny.

Weather

With average high temperatures of 86 °F (30 °C) in Palermo and 90 °F (32 °C) in Catania, July is the second-hottest month of the year in Sicily after August. As a result, even in hilly regions like Ragusa, temperatures frequently don't drop until you ascend over the 1,500-foot level. If you plan to drive inland, keep in mind that the sea air cools the heat. Ragusa averages 90 °F (32 °C) during the hottest portion of the day, but Prizzi, at 3,300 ft (1,000 m), only experiences a high of 81 °F (27 °C). In addition, when the sirocco winds, a searing wind from Africa, are blowing, temperatures in Prizzi can reach 95-97°F (35-36°C).

Pack light clothing and sunscreen because the water is a scorching 77 degrees Fahrenheit (25 degrees Celsius) right now.

Something to Do

A great option to avoid the masses of tourists in the beach-loving month of July is to embark on a sailing trip from Milazzo to the

Aeolian Islands, pausing sometimes for a swim and some exploring, like at the black sands of Mulberry Beach on Vulcano Island. The Aegadi Islands, which are off the coast of Trapani and each have their own wonderful cities, gorgeous beaches, and amazing marine life just waiting to be discovered, are another option. You can take a cruise through and around them.

Another way to escape crowds is to take a picnic and hike to a beach that is less busy. On the south coast of Sciacca, there are two beaches with pine forests: Eraclea Minoa and Torre Salsa.

August

In Sicily, the exciting and pricey season finishes in August. The weather is sunny and hot, perfect for beach days and all things linked to watersports, but you will have to contend with the hordes of both domestic and foreign tourists. However, don't let it demoralize you because this guide will outline what to do and where to go.

Weather

Apart from that, the daily average temperatures of Messina, Palermo, and Syracuse are 88°F (31°C) and 90°F (32°C), respectively.

Bring your swimsuit, sunscreen, and perhaps some light clothing for the evenings when it gets cool, especially if you go inland

and stop in a town that is higher than 1,500 feet. It goes without saying that you should do this (4,921 m). Prizzi, for instance, records a normal range of 63-81 F. (17-27 C). Remember that temperatures are hotter inland when there is little to no sea wind, such as in Ragusa where the average high temperature is 90 °F (32 °C), below 1,000 feet (3,280 m).

Something to Do

If you happen to be in Sicily on August 14, make your way to the coast for a beautiful display of bonfires on every beach and take part in the festivities, which include all-night dancing and partying. If you're visiting Sicily for the sun and waves, put on your swimsuit, look for a towel, and go to the beach. Rent a beach chair at one of the several lidos, but if you want to pick a stretch of sand that is a bit less crowded; you should arrive early in the day or later in the afternoon (about 5 pm).

To choose a beach that meets your needs for a variety of activities like surfing, kayaking, sailing, snorkeling, and scuba diving, visit any nearby beach. Adrenaline junkies might want to think about exploring the Alcantara River and Gorge region if they're looking for a pleasant and relaxing activity. Put your kit on and body raft down the river, stopping to go hiking and swimming.

And in late August, the island-wide grape harvest begins. Drive through the vineyard-dotted landscape of the west coast, stop at a few cantinas in Marsala, and sample some of the fortified wine produced there. There is also the well-known Bianco d'Alcamo from the area between Alcamo and Trapani, in addition to Syrah and Etna Rosso from the fertile volcanic soil of Mount Etna's slopes. If you can't make it to the Aeolian or Pantelleria islands, sip a glass of Malvasia or Passito di Pantelleria, their respective red wines.

September

September is the best month to travel to Sicily because the weather is still pleasant and there aren't as many people. If you're searching for a deal, check near the end of the month because there are so many things to do, including outdoor activities, cultural events, and wine and culinary festivals.

Weather

Sicily's opening in two to three weeks of September feels like a continuation of July and August. However, by the middle of the month, the evenings are cooler and rain is beginning to fall, ushering in the wet season of the fall and winter. Having said that, there may only be two inches of rain this month, so remember to pack your summer clothing along with lighter layers and an umbrella.

While Catania in the east has a range of 63-84 °F (17-29 °C), Palermo, Messina, and Syracuse all have temperatures between

68 and 82 °F (20 and 28 °C). The temperature will be cooler inland in the hills and mountains, more so as you ascend in height. Ragusa has temperatures between 61 and 82 °F (16 to 28 °C) at 1,600 feet (500 m), whereas Prizzi experiences temperatures between 57 and 73 °F (14 to 23 °C) at 3,300 feet (1,000 m).

Something to Do

September offers a plethora of opportunities to enjoy outdoor activities, cultural events, and wine and cuisine festivals. Hazelnuts and almonds are plentiful and appear in many Sagres as the wine and olive harvest proceeds. Other famous events include San Vito Lo Capo's Couscous Fest, which features live music and couscous from throughout the world.

The Pistachio Festival is held in Bronte, which lies west of Taormina, while ViniMilo, an occasion honoring the region's wine, is held in Milo on the slopes of Mount Etna. Enjoy themed meals, winery tours, guided tastings, and seminars before making your way to Cefalù in the central north for a serving or two of dessert. Three days of freshly churned ice cream are offered here as part of the Sherbeth Festival celebration.

Because the weather is less unpleasant and the crowds are starting to thin out, September is a good time to travel to significant locations that would otherwise be challenging to explore (especially toward the middle of the month). You should be informed of the various festivities taking place, though. View the baroque villages, cities, and architecture, as well as the dispersed archaeological sites. If you happen to be on the southern side, stop at the Selinunte archaeological park, the Valley of the Temples in Agrigento, and Villa Romana del Casale in Piazza Armerina.

Take advantage of the pleasant weather by hiking, biking, and climbing in the Madonie and Nebrodi mountains, which are popular with outdoor lovers.

Of course, if you have the confidence, you can even climb Mount Etna's active volcano. Alternately, don your swimming gear and go diving or snorkeling to discover the incredible marine life off the coast of the Aegadi Islands. Visit Ustica Island's greatest marine reserve or take a surfing class in Catania or Cefalù.

If you like to unwind on the beach, Sicily boasts a variety of excellent beaches, so you can't go wrong.

October

You may dodge the crowds and explore Sicily's well-known landmarks in October. There are also a lot of harvest celebrations going on, and the weather is nice enough to draw beachgoers.

Weather

October is pleasantly cool in Sicily. Even though the weather is pleasant and warm, there are more rainstorms, windstorms, and shorter days than usual. In Sicily, most coastal towns experience temperatures that are comparable to Palermo's average high of 75 degrees Fahrenheit (24 degrees Celsius), plus or minus a few degrees. The sea is alluring even at 73°F (23°C). On days when the sirocco blows in from Africa, temperatures also climb, adding to the pleasure of going to the beach.

In the heart of the island, which is made up of hills and mountains, temperatures frequently range from 10 to 17 degrees Celsius (10 to 50 degrees Fahrenheit) in Prizzi and Enna to 12 and 22 degrees Celsius (12 to 72 degrees Fahrenheit) in Ragusa and Caltanissetta.

Something to Do

Sicily's towns and cities hold seasonal food festivals, which makes it the perfect time to indulge in mouthwatering Italian fare like artisanal cheeses, olive oils, chestnuts, and prickly pears. Check out their weekly Sagre, which contains locally produced items including apples, honey, chestnuts, mushrooms, and wine, if you're in the Mount Etna region on a Sunday. To experience something a little more unique, go to the tiny village of Belpasso during their Ficus Indica Festival.

While the weather is nice, go hiking in the Madonie Regional Natural Park by picking from a variety of paths that range in length and difficulty. You should visit Castelbuono to mingle with the locals and take part in their yearly mushroom hunt in addition to seeing the fall foliage. Keep to the east coast and go trekking on Mount Etna for a different, possibly more obvious, choice. You can reach the peak by utilizing a combination of a cable car, a four-wheel-drive vehicle, and foot.

November

November is still a terrific month for seeing urban and cultural sites as well as maybe spending a day at the beach, despite the weather being a little rainier than the rest of the year. The beginning of the wine season in November is also signaled by St. Martin's Day, which opens a number of events honoring seasonal fare and, of course, wine.

Weather

November is among the wettest months of the year (next to December). A few inches of rain are forecast for Sicily this month, and the interior of the island is expected to experience fog at higher elevations. Temperatures along the coast in cities like Palermo and Cefalù in the north, Trapani in the west, and Catania in the east coast frequently fluctuate from 50 to 68 degrees Fahrenheit due to Sicily's primarily mild Mediterranean climate. Swimming in the ocean is not uncommon when near the shore because the water there is typically 69 F (21 C) warmer than the air.

The interior hills and mountains of Sicily naturally experience milder temperatures, with typical lows of 48 °F (9 °C) and highs of 64 °F (18 °C) in Ragusa and colder yet in Prizzi at a higher height (43-54 °F/6-12 °C). However, this difference is most obvious at night. You should pack warmer clothes and a waterproof jacket in addition to your just-in-case swimsuit due to the unpredictability of the weather.

Something to Do

Come to the south shore if the weather is nice to brave a swim or simply relax on one of the many beaches with fewer people around. And if the rains hold off, exploring Sicily's numerous important archaeological sites is absolutely imperative. If you're in the southwest, go to Selinunte's archaeological park to witness spectacular ancient Greek ruins; the Temple of Hera is the most well-known location there.

Wine lovers should time their travel to fall on November 11, St. Martin's Day, when young wine is ready to be sipped and festivities abound with wine tastings and seasonal fare. Because Taormina is the largest island in the Mediterranean, it is best to concentrate on a single wine region. If you have a rental car, take a lovely journey through the Nebrodi mountains' hills to the small town of Castell'Umberto for a spectacular St. Martin's Day celebration. Cheer on contestants rolling barrels while sipping wine in a festive setting and eating local chestnuts and mushrooms.

In addition, if the weather does turn bad, make the most of the downtime by exploring Sicily's distinctive culinary legacy, a blend of tastes influenced by the island's lengthy history of Greek, Arab, and Norman occupation. For a taste of Sicily's native black swine, try Sicilian black pig or pasta with sardines, a national sweet-and-sour dish that mixes wild fennel and North African ingredients like pine nuts, saffron, and dried fruit. You can also go to farms that specialize in growing Maialino Nero, where the acorn, olive, and carob-studded meadows produce sensational-tasting sausage.

Beyond San Martino cookies, there is the Chocolate Festival in Modica to think about, where the renowned chocolate is still made using recipes from the sixteenth century. As a result of the November rains, the pastures become greener, enabling grazing sheep to produce the milk required to make ricotta, the main component of cannoli and cassata (Sicilian cheesecake).

December

It is more affordable to travel during the winter because hotel and airfare rates are lower. The slower pace of winter and the lack of tourists may make it easier to get to know the locals intimately. During the winter, a lot of diamonds can be discovered. Sicily's winter season offers far more than most

71

tourists realize, including culinary delights like the sea urchin harvest season in February and skiing on Mount Etna.

Sicily's festive villages and cities welcome visitors in December who want to celebrate Christmas and New Year's. A great month for discovering remote ancient Greek and Roman monuments, enjoying exquisite Sicilian cuisine, and browsing Christmas markets.

December is the wettest month for weather in Sicily, which is gloomy with sporadic brightening. 52- and 61-degrees Fahrenheit (11 and 16 degrees Celsius) are the island's typical low and high temperatures, with the interior hills of the island experiencing cooler temperatures and occasionally seeing snow during cold spells. The amount of precipitation in mountainous places above 3,300 feet (1,000 m) might be excessive on occasion. Bring an umbrella, sunglasses, warm clothing, and winter gear if you're headed to the mountains.

The very courageous may decide to carry their swimsuit since swimming is still allowed at water temperatures of 64 F (18 C).

Something to Do

Even if it's still warm enough to wear a swimsuit, December is more suited for discovering local customs and taking part in land-based activities, especially since the large crowds of tourists have left. Discover some of the world's most significant archaeological sites. Explore the numerous Greek and Roman archaeological sites that are scattered throughout the island, such as the expansive Selinunte archaeological park, the imposing ridgetop temples of the Valley of the Temples in Agrigento, and the exquisitely preserved and extraordinarily varied mosaics in Villa Romana del Casale. If you want to see a mixture of Greek and Roman ruins while you're in Syracuse, go to the Neapolis Archaeological Park.

As Christmas approaches, each hamlet, village, and city on the island hosts its own festive Christmas market. Wherever you go, sample regional specialties like zabaglione, a Marsala wine-based dessert, and buccellati, a giant circular cookie stuffed with nuts like almonds and pistachios and other dried fruits. While shopping for the appropriate gift or souvenir. In Palermo, the Politeama Theater's Piazza Unita d'Italia is a well-managed tangle of food and handicraft booths. Erice, a medieval mountainside hamlet that changes into a Christmas paradise with stunning carnivals, concerts, and parades practically every day, offers a more immersive experience.

As the month of December comes to an end, focus shifts from Christmas to New Year's Eve celebrations. Most of the local towns, including Palermo, Catania, and Messina, celebrate the New Year with live performances by local and foreign musicians, fireworks, and food. If you plan to eat out, make reservations in advance and prepare for a classic Cenone multi-course meal (feast). Undoubtedly, lentils will be offered since they are symbolic of wealth and prosperity.

For a unique way to ring in the New Year, go on a guided climb to the active volcano Stromboli on the Aeolian Islands if the weather permits. Even Stromboli itself might put on a fireworks display.

There are a variety of prime periods to visit Sicily depending on what each traveler intends to gain out of their vacation. The most beautiful times of year in this region are early and late summer, but there is still a lot of beauty to be seen in the less popular months. If you want some quiet time, stay away from the busiest travel period. If you can't get enough of the outdoor activities offered here, don't be afraid to brave the throng and take a little bit of that paradise home.

Chapter 4:

Itineraries

One week itinerary

If you have one week to explore Sicily, here's a suggested itinerary that covers some of the highlights of the island:

Day 1: Palermo

- Arrive at Palermo, Sicily's capital.
- Visit Palermo's historic center to see sights including the Norman Palace, Quattro Canti, and the Palermo Cathedral.
- Explore the bustling markets like the Vucciria or Ballar while eating some of the regional fare.

Day 2: Monreale and Cefalù

- Visit Monreale for the day; it's a neighbouring town known for its magnificent cathedral and ornate mosaics.
- After seeing Monreale, proceed to Cefalù, a charming seaside town renowned for its lovely beach and medieval district.
- Visit Cefalù's lovely shops in the afternoon and take in the scenery from La Rocca, a rocky point.

Day 3: Agrigento and Valley of the Temples

- Visit the Valley of the Temples in Agrigento, a UNESCO World Heritage site with well-preserved Greek remains.
- View the great Greek temples, such as the Temple of Concordia and the Temple of Juno, while exploring the archaeological park.

Day 4: Syracuse and Ortigia

- Consider visiting Syracuse, a storied city with a strong Greek and Roman past.
- Visit sites including the Temple of Apollo, the Fountain of Arethusa, and the Piazza Duomo while exploring the island of Ortigia, the historical center of Syracuse.
- Wander around Ortigia's lovely streets and take in the lively ambiance..

Day 5: Mount Etna and Taormina

- Visit Mount Etna, one of the most active volcanoes in the world, for the day.
- Take a trip, explore the lowest parts of the volcano, and discover its geology and history.
- After that, travel to Taormina, a stunning town that is set on a hill overlooking the sea.
- Explore Taormina's gorgeous streets and the historic Greek Theater.

Day 6: Catania

- Visit Catania, the second-largest city in Sicily, which is renowned for its vivacious atmosphere and Baroque architecture.
- Discover the historic core and its landmarks, including the Fontana dell'Elefante and Piazza del Duomo.
- La Pescheria, a bustling fish market where you may sample the regional cuisine, should not be missed.

Day 7: Trapani and Erice

- Visit Trapani, a seaside city on the westernmost point of Sicily.
- Take a cable car up to the mountaintop medieval village of Erice for sweeping views of the surroundings.

- Visit the Castle of Venus, stroll through the quaint streets of Erice, and take in the peace and quiet of this historic settlement.

five days itinerary

If you have five days to explore Sicily, here's a suggested itinerary that will allow you to experience some of the highlights of the island:

Day 1: Palermo

- Arrive at Palermo, Sicily's capital.
- Visit the city's historic district, which is renowned for its fusion of architectural styles influenced by several civilizations, during the course of the day.
- Explore the Palermo Cathedral, the Royal Palace, and the Baroque square of Quattro Canti.
- Visit the busy markets in Ballar or Vucciria to enjoy the cuisine of the region.
- Dine at a classic Sicilian restaurant in the evening.

Day 2: Agrigento and Valley of the Temples

- Visit Agrigento, which is situated on Sicily's southern coast, for the day.
- A UNESCO World Heritage site with well-preserved Greek ruins is the Valley of the Temples.

- Discover the famous Temple of Concordia and Temple of Juno, as well as the rest of the archaeological park.
- Take in the expansive vistas of the surrounding landscape.
- After dark, return to Palermo.

Day 3: Cefalù and Taormina

- Travel to Cefalù, a lovely beach village east of Palermo.
- Visit the beautiful Cefalù Cathedral, stroll around the medieval district, and unwind on the white-sand beaches.
- After that, travel to Taormina, which is located on Sicily's eastern coast.
- Visit the historic Greek Theater, stroll through the charming village, and take in Mount Etna's vistas.
- Dine at a nearby restaurant in the evening.

Day 4: Mount Etna and Catania

- Visit Mount Etna, the tallest active volcano in Europe, on a day trip.
- Discover the lava flows, craters, and picturesque vistas that the volcano has to offer.
- To get to higher elevations, take a guided tour or ride a cable car.
- Following that, proceed to Catania.
- Visit the Piazza del Duomo, stroll through Catania's ancient district, and indulge in some regional specialties.
- Go back to your lodging in Catania or Taormina.

Day 5: Syracuse and Ortigia Island

- On Sicily's southeast coast, explore the historic city of Syracuse.
- Discover the Greek Theater and the Ear of Dionysius in the Neapolis archaeological park.
- Visit Ortigia Island, which is where Syracuse's ancient center is located.
- Visit the Syracuse Cathedral, stroll through the winding alleyways, and take in the lovely shoreline.
- If you have the time, think about taking a boat tour of Ortigia or unwinding at a local beach.
- Return to your lodging in the evening.

A weekend itinerary

A weekend vacation to Sicily is a fantastic way to experience the island's fascinating history, stunning scenery, and delectable cuisine. To help you make the most of your weekend in Sicily, here is a suggested itinerary:

Day 1:

Morning:

- Depending on your flight options, arrive at either the Palermo or Catania Fontanarossa airports.

- Depending on where you landed, either rent a car or take a cab to get to your lodging in Catania or Palermo..

Afternoon:

- Visit the Piazza del Duomo in Catania's historic center to see the majestic Catania Cathedral and the Fontana dell'Elefante.
- La Pescheria, a lively fish market, can be explored.
- Take a leisurely stroll through Catania's main retail strip, Via Etnea, which is surrounded by stores, cafes, and stunning architecture.

Evening:

- Dine on authentic Sicilian fare in a neighborhood eatery in Catania, where you can sample specialties like arancini and pasta alla Norma.

Day 2:

Morning:

- Head to Mount Etna, Europe's tallest active volcano:
- Visit the Etna Visitor Center and make arrangements for a cable car or jeep excursion to explore the volcano's slopes and craters, or go on a guided tour.
- Take in the breathtaking surroundings while learning about the region's geological past.

Afternoon:

- Visit the lovely hilltop village of Taormina, which is renowned for its breathtaking vistas and ancient Greek theater:
- Visit the Greek Theater, which offers sweeping views of the Ionian Sea and Mount Etna, and stroll through the old district.
- Explore the charming streets that are lined with shops, cafes, and gelato stores.
- Visit Villa Comunale's lovely grounds or unwind on Isola Bella's breathtaking beaches.

Evening:

- While soaking in the scenery and indulging in regional seafood delicacies, have a romantic meal in Taormina.

Day 3:

Morning:

- Depart from Catania or Palermo, depending on where you are staying, and head to Syracuse (Siracusa):
- Explore the amazing ancient Greek and Roman monuments in Neapolis' archaeological park, which includes the Greek Theater, the Ear of Dionysius, and the Roman Amphitheater.

- Discover Ortygia Island, Syracuse's historical core, with its quaint, winding lanes, Baroque structures, and breathtaking Piazza Duomo.

Afternoon:

- If you have the time, you should visit Noto, a town renowned for its exquisitely preserved Baroque buildings and a UNESCO World Heritage Site.
- Alternately, you can unwind on the neighboring beaches or see additional historical places in Syracuse throughout the day.

Evening:

- Depending on where you left from, go back to Catania or Palermo for your next destination or overnight stay.

Please be aware that this schedule is predicated on you having a car available. You might need to modify the plan to take into account travel timings and availability if you prefer public transportation. Additionally, it's a good idea to verify the availability and opening times of restaurants and activities beforehand because they may change depending on the season.

Chapter 5:
Affordable Hotels And
Restaurants In Sicily

Places to Stay

Hotel Palazzo Sitano, Palermo

The hotel is situated at 114 Via Vittorio Emanuele, Palermo, Sicily, 90133. The Palermo historic center is home to this beautiful 18th-century Baroque townhouse. Just 150 meters from Piazza Marina, its modern rooms provide flat-screen satellite TV.

Parquet floors and minibars can be found in every room at Palazzo Sitano. There is a private bathroom in each room. There are many balconies. The Nintendo Wii in the foyer is available to guests for free use for 30 minutes each day. Fresh fruit, vegetables, and cheeses are all included in the variety free buffet breakfast. Buses that connect you to Palermo Railway Station stop immediately outside the Palazzo Sitano Hotel. It takes 15 minutes to walk to the harbor.

Reservations start at €124. Children continue to be free.

Hotel Letizia, Palermo

Hotel Letizia, also in Palermo, is situated on Via dei Bottai in the city's famed La Kalsa neighborhood. Persian carpets cover the parquet floors, the ceilings are rustically vaulted, and the bedspreads are luxurious. Modern comforts coexist with antique furniture. A half-block separates you from downtown Palermo. Corso Vittorio Emanuele and the lovely, café-lined Piazza Marina are also accessible on foot. A big suite with a patio costs €200, and rooms start at €155 per night.

Casale del Principe, Monreale

You can stay at Casale del Principe in Monreale, which is located a half-hour drive from Palermo. The former monastery that has been converted to a farm now offers culinary and ceramics classes, horseback riding, and archery. The hotel produces its own wine, marmalades, pastries, and veggies. A neighbor makes cheeses.

You can stroll through fruit orchards, vineyards, olive groves, and poppy farms. For €27, guests may enjoy a four-course supper in the hotel restaurant. There are nine rooms for guests. Three of the apartments feature private patios with views of the mountains and Valle dello Jato. Enjoy the 21 nature pathways that local hiking organizations have mapped out and the courtyard fountain. Rent is available for €121.

Hotel Acqua Marina, Ragusa

At 90 euros for a double occupancy, this hotel is reasonably priced if you want to be near the beach. The welcoming, locally managed Hotel Acqua Marina in the province of Ragusa is perched on a crag with a bird's eye view over Donnalucata's lovely beach and offers a great seafood restaurant with sea views to match. Beyond the sand, there is a private area of grass where you can sunbathe, and the full, daily breakfast is served on the upstairs sundeck. At the other end of the beach, there is an outdoor market where farmers sell their produce off of trucks for visitors who want to take a stroll. The hotel is not far from Scicli, an exquisite inland baroque village.

Holland International Rooms, Catania

The most expensive component of travel is lodging. The negative impact of the euro exchange is also felt by travelers. Why not try a hostel if cost-effectiveness in your accommodations is important?

At Via Vittorio Emanuele II, 8, Catania, Catania, you can find Holland International Rooms. It is housed in a restored antique 18th-century structure in Catania's historic district. Original frescoes that graced the room ceilings still exist. Some of the rooms in the hostel have views of the Mediterranean while others are quieter and are located in a large courtyard.

The distance to the bus stop and train station is three minutes by foot. You may plan trips to Mount Etna, Syracuse, and Taormina from here. Restaurants, bars, and pizzerias can be reached on foot in a short time. The bedrooms have air conditioning. Wi-Fi and satellite TV are available.

Rent for a room is 20 euros per night.

Renda Appartamenti, Trapani

You may choose to stay in Renda Appartamenti if an apartment is more to your taste. Located in Trapani at Via G.B. Fardella. Rent for this two-star, fully furnished condo in Canada is €100 per night. This 1900 structure has undergone remodeling. It is located in Trapani on a busy street. The Museo di Preistoria e del Mare and Museo Regionale Conte Agostino Pepoli are both accessible by foot from the flat. Visitors can take in Sant Agostino Church or meander through the charming cobblestone lanes to nearby medieval castles. Hikers can explore the countryside, and they can also visit nearby markets.

Places to Eat & Drink

In Sicily, as in other locations, eating out for lunch is far less expensive than doing so for evening. There are several places in Palermo with reasonable prices that serve a lot of home-cooked meals. Trattoria Da Pino, a nearby trattoria, is one of them.

Trattoria Da Pino, Palermo

Palermo 90139, via dello Spezio 6, is where you may find it. A well-known local restaurant is called Da Pino. Its highlights include superb and ample meat- and fish-based cuisine. One of the restaurant's peculiarities is that half portions can be ordered, which is great for dieters. Along with the meatballs, sword fish, prawns, and grilled meats, the white Bolognese pasta is a particular fan favorite.

Restaurant Antico Baglio Santo Pietro, Caltagirone

The best deal in all of Sicily may be found at this restaurant, which is situated on Piazzetta del Borgo in Caltagirone. A nice supper may be had for as little as 25 euros. For lunch, you can also order a variety of pizzas.

Agritursimo Antico Baglio, Caltagirone

Agriturismo Antico Baglio is yet another outstanding Italian restaurant in Caltagirone. The restaurant is situated on San Pietro and offers evening meals for 33 to 39 euros. Eat lunch outside on the patio.

Caffe Mamma Caura, Marsala

Contrada de Ettore Ingersa, also referred to as Caffe Mamma Caura by the locals, is a fantastic restaurant if you are in or around Marsala. This is a budget-friendly café by the water close to the Mozia ferry. The terrace has a view of windmills and saltpans. Mamma Cuara's morning's cooking is listed on a board as the menu. Arancini, spherical, orange-sized risotto fritters packed with ricotta and spinach or ham and cheese, are among the specialties.

Palermo Markets

Some of the best cheap takeout cuisine can be found here. Along with the fruit and vegetables, you can eat Purpu (chopped and boiled octopus) and cooked artichokes. Pani cu' la meuza stands may be found at every market. These bread rolls are stuffed with sautéed beef or tripe and topped with fresh ricotta and caciocavallo cheese. Vicciria, located off Via Roma between Corso Vittorio Emanuele and the San Domenico church, is home to the best market. Get some lunch and eat outside while enjoying the freshest food available anyplace in a park or at a table by the side of the road.

Chapter 6:

Local Cuisine In Sicily

Sicily, an enchanting island located off the coast of southern Italy, is renowned for its rich culinary heritage. Sicilian cuisine is a unique fusion of Mediterranean flavors, influenced by Greek, Arab, Norman, and Spanish cultures. The island boasts a plethora of delicious dishes that showcase the freshest local ingredients. Here are the top 10 must-try Italian cuisines in Sicily, along with some recommended places to find them:

1. Arancini: Arancini are famous rice balls from Sicily that are often stuffed with peas, mozzarella cheese, and ragù (meat sauce). These golden-fried treats come in a variety of flavors. "Bar Touring" in Palermo is a suggested location to try arancini.

2. Spaghetti alla Norma: Originally from Catania, pasta alla Norma is a traditional Sicilian meal. Short pasta (often rigatoni or penne) is mixed in a tomato, eggplant, basil, and ricotta salata sauce (a salty cheese). For a taste of the real thing, go to "Trattoria da Nino" in Catania.

3. Cannoli: Ricotta cheese cream filling is inside these delectable pastries known as cannoli. Traditional flavorings for the crispy shell include Marsala wine. Go to "Pasticceria Cappello" in Palermo for the best cannoli in Sicily.

4. Sicilian eggplant dish called caponata is produced by frying chopped eggplants with celery, onions, capers, olives, and a sweet-and-sour sauce. Visit Osteria Ballar in Palermo and get this tasty dish.

5. Panelle: Panelle are Sicilian street snack that are made of chickpeas. They are prepared using a batter of chickpea flour, water, parsley, and seasonings, which is then perfectly deep-fried. In Palermo, go to "Friggitoria Cucinotta" for some delectable panelle.

6. Pasta con le Sarde: Sardines, wild fennel, raisins, pine nuts, and saffron are all ingredients in this pasta recipe. It showcases the variety of tastes found in Sicilian cuisine and is a specialty of Palermo. Try it in Palermo at "Antica Focacceria San Francesco."

7. A cool frozen treat called granita is produced from sugar, water, and a variety of tastes like lemon, almond,

pistachio, or coffee. Visit "Caffè Sicilia" in Noto for a genuine granita experience.

8. Spaghetti ai Ricci di Mare: For those who enjoy shellfish, there is this dish. It consists of spaghetti tossed in a sauce consisting of olive oil, garlic, chili flakes, and sea urchin roe. Syracuse's "Ristorante Don Camillo" is a well-known location to sample this delicacy.

9. Busiate alla Trapanese: Trapani is known for its own brand of pasta known as busiate alla Trapanese. It comes with a tomato, garlic, almond, basil, and pecorino cheese sauce. The Trapani restaurant "Osteria La Bettolaccia" is a fantastic place to sample this local delicacy.

10. Sfincione: A thick, spongy Sicilian-style pizza topped with tomato sauce, onions, anchovies, and breadcrumbs is known as sfincione. It can be obtained at the "Antica Focacceria San Francesco" in Palermo, which is a neighborhood favorite.

Chapter 7:

Nightlife And Festivals In Sicily

The beautiful island of Sicily awakens when the sun begins to set, embracing its renowned vivid and alluring nightlife. The streets come to life with a kaleidoscope of colors, pulsing energy, and an overpowering sense of exhilaration. Let me describe the nightlife in Sicily to you in detail.

You will find yourself immersed in a world where ancient history and contemporary merriment effortlessly coexist as you travel into Palermo, the center of Sicily. You are drawn to the bustling alleys lined with lovely trattorias and boisterous bars by the alluring aromas of Sicilian food that fill the air.

You are enticed to follow the songs by the alluring sounds of live music that are spilling out onto the cobblestone streets. You are at Piazza San Domenico, a lively square with elaborate fountains and a lovely glow from the streetlights. As the evening progresses, residents and tourists mingle here, sharing jokes and stories.

Later on in the evening, Syracuse's Ortigia historic quarter invites you with its enduring appeal. A cozy environment that is ideal for exploration is created by the small passageways that wind around historic structures. The doors of hip bars and fashionable clubs fly open as you go along the shoreline to let in the contagious sounds of live DJs and skilled musicians.

You travel to Taormina, a coastal town located high on a hill overlooking the azure Mediterranean Sea, after leaving the city behind. You may watch stunning opera or theatrical shows under a starry Sicilian sky at the town's famed Teatro Antico, which transforms into a stage for mesmerizing outdoor performances.

The lovely village of Cefalù is there for you if you're looking for a more laid-back and bohemian setting. As the evening wears on, the sleepy streets become a hive of creativity, with energetic street performers exhibiting their skills and small wine bars inviting you to have a glass of Sicilian wine while listening to the soothing sounds of local musicians.

The beach clubs and resorts along the coast of Sicily provide a distinctive experience, expanding the island's nightlife beyond its cities and villages. You may dance the night away on sandy beaches in locations like Mondello and Giardini Naxos while taking in the sparkling lights and soft lapping of the waves.

The nightlife in Sicily is renowned for its love of food. You may savor mouthwatering regional specialties like arancini, cannoli, and fresh seafood dishes at vibrant street food markets and upscale restaurants while sipping a fragrant glass of Sicilian wine or a cool limoncello.

You can find yourself mesmerized by the lingering allure of the Sicilian night as dawn draws near. Sicily's nightlife will leave you with indelible memories of a captivating and vivacious island that never sleeps, whether you decide to immerse yourself in the lively streets of Palermo, the medieval charm of Syracuse, or the laid-back beachfront environment.

Festivals

These celebrations give locals and visitors a chance to gather together and celebrate while showcasing the island's rich cultural heritage. The following list of well-known Sicilian festivals includes their typical dates, as well as the events that mark them:

1. One of Sicily's most significant religious celebrations, **the Feast of Saint Agatha** (Festa di Sant'Agata) is held in Catania to commemorate Saint Agatha, the city's patron saint. It lasts from February 3rd to February 5th. The celebration includes religious processions, such as the

street procession of the saint's relics. Participants dress in traditional attire and participate in prayers and rituals throughout this intensely spiritual and emotional occasion.

2. Acireale, a town close to Catania, holds one of Sicily's most renowned and vibrant carnivals every February, known as the **Carnival of Acireale** (Carnevale di Acireale). A procession with elaborately decorated floats, traditional music, dancing, and costumed performers are all part of the event. Visitors can take in the festive mood, eat the local street food, and take pleasure in the bustling ambiance.

3. **Almond Blossom Festival** (Sagra del Mandorlo in Fiore) - February/March: In Agrigento, in the southern region of Sicily, the Almond Blossom Festival is held. When the almond trees blossom and cover the landscape in a stunning blanket of white and pink flowers, it marks the beginning of spring. The celebration includes dancing, music, art displays, and traditional Sicilian food, with an emphasis on recipes that include almonds.

4. **The Feast of Saint Rosalia** (Festa di Santa Rosalia) is a significant religious celebration celebrated in Palermo to honor the city's patron saint. It takes place on July 14 and 15. During the celebration, the saint's statue is carried through Palermo's streets while being accompanied by musicians and pyrotechnics. A spectacular fireworks show

over the port that lights up the night sky marks the event's conclusion.

5. September: San Vito lo Capo, a coastal town in northwest Sicily, hosts **the Cous Cous Fest**, an annual international food event. This festival showcases a variety of couscous dishes made in distinct Mediterranean ways to honor Sicily's rich cultural diversity. Food tastings, cooking demonstrations, live music, and cultural performances are available to visitors.

6. **Infiorata di Noto** is a distinctive floral festival conducted in the town of Noto, which is renowned for its breathtaking Baroque architecture. It takes place in May or June. The streets of Noto are decorated with elaborate and vibrant floral carpets throughout the festival, creating magnificent shapes and patterns. Along with concerts and traditional Sicilian music and dance acts, the festival also features art exhibits.

These are only a few of the numerous festivals that are observed throughout Sicily. Each festival offers a different experience, fusing musical performances, artistic displays, and religious traditions. The times shown are an estimate, and it's always a good idea to double-check each festival's precise dates because they sometimes change a little bit from year to year.

Chapter 8:

Shopping And Souvenirs In Sicily

Sicily offers a wide variety of shopping opportunities to suit a variety of tastes and price ranges. Sicily has something for everyone, from traditional goods and handicrafts to designer labels and upscale clothing. Here are some of Sicily's well-liked tourist retail areas:

1. Palermo: Palermo, the capital of Sicily, offers a wide variety of retail options. For upscale clothing boutiques, visit Via della Libertà and Via Ruggero Settimo. For traditional goods, fresh vegetables, and street cuisine, visit local markets like Vucciria, Ballar, and Capo.

2. Catania: Shops, boutiques, and department stores abound on the city's busy streets. The main retail district is located in Via Etnea, where you can find clothing stores, gift shops, and other establishments. It's also worthwhile to visit the renowned fish market, La Pescheria.

3. Taormina: This charming town is well-known for its posh shopping district. The main thoroughfare, Corso Umberto, is lined with designer shops, jewelry stores, and art galleries. The neighborhood artisan stores that sell ceramics, lace, and handmade goods are not to be missed.

4. Siracusa: Look for artisan stores selling regional delicacies, ceramics, and traditional crafts along the winding lanes of Ortigia, the city's old district. The Ortigia Market is a fantastic location to find seasonal foods, spices, and fresh fruit.

5. Agrigento: Although known for its historic ruins, Agrigento also provides retail options. The main shopping district, Via Atenea, is home to a variety of high-end retailers, independent boutiques, and artisanal studios.

6. Caltagirone is the perfect location to browse for distinctive pottery and home furnishings because it is well-known for its wonderful ceramics. The town is teeming with ceramic studios and shops where you can see the art in action.

7. Visit Marsala, which is known for its fortified wine, if you enjoy wine. Explore the wine cellars and specialty stores to taste and buy various sorts of Marsala wine.

Always verify the store hours before visiting, as many may close for a short time in the late afternoon. Also remember that some smaller shops and markets might only take cash, so it's a good idea to have some euros on hand.

Souvenirs

Here are some popular souvenirs you can find in Sicily and where to buy them:

1. Pottery: The vivid colors and intricate patterns of Sicilian ceramics are well-known. Look for hand-painted dishes, bowls, tiles, and decorative items with iconic designs like Sicilian carts, flowers, and lemons. Ceramic shops and workshops can be found in the cities of Taormina, Santo Stefano di Camastra, and Caltagirone.
2. Puppets Siciliani (Sicilian Puppets): The legacy of puppet theater in Sicily includes these historic marionettes. They are made by hand and frequently include knights, kings, and other mythical figures from Sicilian history and folklore. In Palermo and Catania, you may find them in speciality stores and marketplaces.
3. Sicilian cart miniatures, or carretto: These miniatures are exquisitely painted and embellished with complex

ornaments, drawing inspiration from the vibrant carts that were once utilized for transportation. They make wonderful collectibles or ornamental things. You may find them all across Sicily in artisanal stores and markets.

4. Gourmet items from Sicily: Sicily is well-known for its mouthwatering cuisine offerings. Extra virgin olive oil, Sicilian sea salt, pistachios, almond pastries, honey, and Sicilian wines are just a few examples of the many souvenirs available. For genuine and premium goods, go to local markets, specialty food shops, or farms in cities like Marsala, Ragusa, and Modica.

5. Handwoven Textiles: Tablecloths, runners, and towels made in Sicily are renowned for their elaborate patterns and vivid colors. They frequently use traditional designs like Sicilian carts or "pupi" (marionettes). Look for them at street markets or artisanal stores, particularly in cities like Palermo, Siracusa, and Agrigento.

6. Sicily is well known for its **coral jewelry**, especially in the town of Trapani. Red coral is used to create a range of items, including necklaces, bracelets, earrings, and pendants. Make sure you buy from trusted merchants who offer genuine coral products.

7. Trinacria Symbol Memorabilia The Trinacria, which represents the island's triangular shape, is a representation of Sicily. It frequently has a Medusa head with wheat ears and a triskelion surrounding it. In souvenir

shops all across Sicily, look for trinacria-inspired trinkets like keychains, magnets, t-shirts, and ceramic tiles.

When shopping for souvenirs in Sicily, consider visiting local markets like the Vucciria Market in Palermo or the Fish Market in Catania. These vibrant markets offer a wide variety of goods, including handicrafts, food products, and souvenirs. Additionally, explore the historic city centers and artisanal shops in popular towns and cities for unique and authentic items.

Remember to buy from reputable sources to ensure the quality and authenticity of your souvenirs.

Conclusion

Sicily is one of those places that may take a lifetime to fully explore. Consider the beautiful beaches you could visit, the surrounding Aegadian Islands, the activities you could partake in, and the boat trips you could take.

The historic coastal towns, historic cities, and archaeological sites would be a maze for architecture fans and history buffs. As is to be expected, Sicily is one of those destinations where you conclude your trip already planning your return.

Sicily is unequaled in its natural and historic beauty, which surpasses that of the entire continent of Europe. When you consider that Sicily also has some of the best Mediterranean beaches and excellent traditional Sicilian cuisine, it is immediately clear why it is Italy's and the rest of Europe's favorite vacation destination.